THE OFFICIAL
HIBERNIAN
FOOTBALL CLUB ANNUAL 2013

Written by David Forsyth
Designed by Jane Massey

A Grange Publication

© 2012. Published by Grange Communications Ltd., Edinburgh, under licence from Hibernian Football Club. Printed in the EU

Photographs © SNSPix

ISBN no. 978-1-908925-07-7

£7.99

Contents

Welcome
to the
Official
2013
HIBERNIAN FC Annual

Chairman's Welcome

We look forward to 2013 with optimism, the Club and fans working together to create a stronger and more prosperous future.

Every Club needs it supporters. The supporters – their passion, commitment, the colour and noise that they bring to the live spectacle that is football – are essential for this most loved of sports. Without the backing of supporters, the spectacle of football is hugely diminished.

All in Scottish football have endured a dramatic few months, but now we need to look ahead and to learn the lessons of the recent past. Football Clubs must live within their means – as families, businesses and other organisations do – if they want to survive and thrive into the future. The alternative path to sane and sustainable stewardship leads, eventually, to crisis and heartbreak.

Hibernian supporters – thousands of them – have told us they want to see sporting success on the pitch, and a sustainably and professionally run Club off it. These are aims your Board and your Club share.

Enjoy the annual – and let's work together to create a brighter future for our Club!

Rod Petrie

Season Review

Season 2011/12 was to prove an emotional roller-coaster for Hibernian supporters, with poor league form accompanied by a run to the final of the Scottish Cup – only for further disappointment to be met.

The season kicked off in **July**, and following an opening day defeat to Celtic at Easter Road the team travelled to Inverness – traditionally an unhappy hunting ground – and returned with three points following a 1-0 win.

August saw defeats suffered in three premier league fixtures, to Kilmarnock, St Mirren and Hearts with only the comfort of a 5-0 cup win against Berwick Rangers to keep fans spirits up.

September was to prove much more positive. Three league draws were achieved against Aberdeen, Dunfermline and Dundee United and also a win, against St Johnstone at Easter Road. However, the highlight of the month was a thrilling penalty shoot-out win (following a 2-2 draw in regulation time) against high-flying Motherwell at Fir Park in the Scottish Communities League Cup.

October again saw fortunes fall, as Hibernian lost out to Celtic in the league cup and also suffered league defeats to Rangers, Motherwell and Celtic. Three points were collected against St Mirren in the league.

In **November**, a solitary point was achieved in the league against Kilmarnock, with losses to Dunfermline and St Johnstone. During the month the Club parted company with manager Colin Calderwood, replaced by Irishman Pat Fenlon.

The tough festive fixture list saw little change in fortunes, with losses in **December** to Rangers, Aberdeen and Dundee United followed by a draw with Inverness, but **January** saw a flurry of incoming transfer activity as the Manager made signings – both longer-term and loans – to steady the ship. That had an immediate impact, following a disappointing New Year derby loss to Hearts, with two wins – against Cowdenbeath in the Scottish Cup and in a vital league match away to Dunfermline, buoyed by a huge and vocal Hibernian support. Two defeats followed, to Rangers and St Johnstone.

MON   FRI   SAT   SUN

30   01

02   07   08

09   14   15

16   21   22

23   28   29

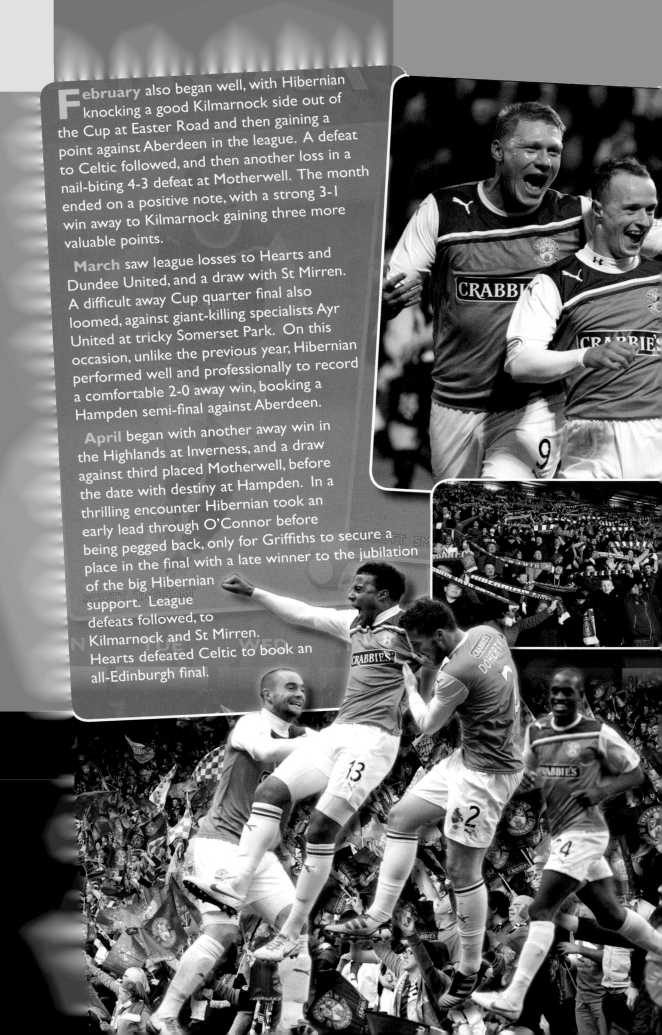

February also began well, with Hibernian knocking a good Kilmarnock side out of the Cup at Easter Road and then gaining a point against Aberdeen in the league. A defeat to Celtic followed, and then another loss in a nail-biting 4-3 defeat at Motherwell. The month ended on a positive note, with a strong 3-1 win away to Kilmarnock gaining three more valuable points.

March saw league losses to Hearts and Dundee United, and a draw with St Mirren. A difficult away Cup quarter final also loomed, against giant-killing specialists Ayr United at tricky Somerset Park. On this occasion, unlike the previous year, Hibernian performed well and professionally to record a comfortable 2-0 away win, booking a Hampden semi-final against Aberdeen.

April began with another away win in the Highlands at Inverness, and a draw against third placed Motherwell, before the date with destiny at Hampden. In a thrilling encounter Hibernian took an early lead through O'Connor before being pegged back, only for Griffiths to secure a place in the final with a late winner to the jubilation of the big Hibernian support. League defeats followed, to Kilmarnock and St Mirren. Hearts defeated Celtic to book an all-Edinburgh final.

M ay the final month of the season began with great promise. An away win at Aberdeen was followed by a crushing defeat of Dunfermline, by 4-0 at Easter Road as the team turned in their home performance of the season. The threat of relegation gone, a much weakened Hibernian side lost narrowly to Inverness in the final league match.

The all-Edinburgh Cup Final was one of colour and noise as fans of both sides travelled to Hampden for the derby dubbed the biggest-ever. Sadly, it was to be a sad and sobering day for Hibernian, with the team performing poorly on the day for the first time in their Cup run, with a 5-1 defeat the outcome.

SEASON QUIZ

⟳ **Name the Manager appointed in November 2011**

⟳ **Which Hibernian-supporting striker joined the Club on loan from Wolves?**

⟳ **Who scored the goals in Hibernian's Cup semi-final win against Aberdeen?**

⟳ **Which player was sent off on his Hibernian debut?**

⟳ **Name the goalkeeper who was the league-cup penalty shoot-out hero against Motherwell?**

⟳ **Pa-Kujabi plays for which national team?**

⟳ **James McPake made his debut for which national side during the season?**

Answers on page 58-59

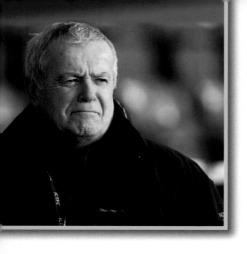

Pat Stanton

Hibernian Hero and The Quiet Man

The term "Legend" is one of the most over-used in football – but just occasionally it is the only term sufficient to describe a player's contribution.

Pat Stanton is, quite simply, a Hibernian legend. Perhaps the biggest Hibs hero of them all – certainly up there with Smith, Johnstone, Reilly, Turnbull and Ormond from the Famous Five and the great goal-scorer Joe Baker. Only Franck Sauzee from the modern era can truly claim the same kind of space in the hearts of supporters.

When "The Quiet Man" speaks, all of the Hibernian family listens.

Pat was always destined to be a Hibernian fan.

He is a distant relative of the Club's first captain, Michael Whelahan and a great nephew of Jimmy Hendren, who signed for the Club in 1911 only to die, prematurely from natural causes, during the First World War.

Pat was born in Edinburgh in 1944, a native of the Niddrie area of the city where he and his mates played boys club football, as well as

being involved in impromptu kickabouts with up to 20 a side. It was a grassroots "system" that saw every lad old enough involved in football, and produced what seemed an endless stream of talented young Scottish players.

Stanton himself was signed by Walter Galbraith in 1961, and was farmed out to junior side Bonnyrigg Rose. In 1963 he made his debut at the tender age of 19, beginning a Hibernian career that would see him turn out almost 400 times in league matches for the Club. His wage was £17 a week. He scored on his debut, against Motherwell. It was to be the first of many big goals for the Club.

At the time of his signing he and the other players had to train where they could find space, often being chased away from parks in the process! As he told reporters: "And this was when we were beating Real Madrid!"

Pat also scored in the 5-0 demolition of Italian giants Napoli and in the League Cup triumph over Celtic in 1972. He also played a pivotal role in the famous New Year's Day victory over Hearts by 7-0 at Tynecastle as part

When "The Quiet Man" speaks, all of the Hibernian family listens.

of the wonderful Turnbull's Tornadoes.

His silverware as a Hibernian player also included two Drybrough Cup wins, and he is often asked why that talented team of the 1970s didn't add more silver to the Easter Road sideboard. The great Celtic 9-in-a-row team stood in their way, of course, but he is philosophical about it and can justly point to the trophies and matches that were won.

Pat was famously described by then Scotland manager Tommy Docherty as a better player than England's World Cup winning skipper, Bobby Moore. Yet his haul of 16 international caps remains far too few to reflect his worth as a player most acknowledge should have won many, many more international honours.

His move to Celtic, with Jackie McNamara coming East as part of the deal, was met with fury by the Hibernian support but it saw him reunited with Jock Stein and sign off on his immaculate career as a player with League and Scottish Cup winners medals. In all, he made 44 appearances for the Hoops

before retiring as a player in 1978, when a testimonial involving the two clubs saw a crowd of 20,000 at Easter Road.

Pat enjoyed a short spell as second-in-command to Alex Ferguson at Aberdeen, and remains in regular contact with the legendary knight of football. He then managed on his own at Cowdenbeath and Dunfermline before taking over at Hibernian in 1982 where he spent two years, signing a number of exciting young players including Mickey Weir, Paul Kane, Gordon Hunter and one John Collins.

In all, Pat scored 51 league goals and 25 in cups. His love affair with the Club remains strong, and he is a regular match-day host. As he told one interviewer: "Some folk have credit cards: my two most important pieces of plastic are my bus pass and my ticket for Easter Road."

> **Every team needs a strong leader on the pitch and James is that – he leads by example and sets high standards.**

The capture of James McPake at the start of the season on a two-year deal was greeted with happiness down Leith way as supporters breathed a sigh of relief that the Club had a captain who was a leader on the pitch.

The centre-half, who played half of last season on loan, proved to be the inspirational defender that the Club had been searching for and his bravery and determination quickly made him a fans favourite.

It also prompted Manager Pat Fenlon to hand James the armband, despite his status as a loan player. Once his loan period was over, the Manager was always determined to get his man.

At the end of June, early in the transfer window, the fans got the news they had been looking for when the Club announced his signature on a two-year deal. James joined from Coventry City, and the Manager's top target had been secured.

James was equally delighted, feeling at home at Hibernian and understanding the nature and scale of the Club: "It's an honour to play for Hibernian and for the Club's supporters. I'm excited to be part of it, and I will play my part in bringing success back."

His capture delighted Pat Fenlon, who said: "Every team needs a strong leader on the pitch and James is that – he leads by example and sets high standards."

- ⚽ **James is aged 28**
- ⚽ **He is 6ft 2 ins tall**
- ⚽ **He has played for Livingston, Morton and Coventry City before joining Hibernian**
- ⚽ **He won his first full cap for Northern Ireland last season against The Netherlands**

The Skipper

CRABBIES

McPAKE

15

QUIZ

➡ **Who was the first Captain of Hibernian?**

➡ **Name the Manager and Captain of Turnbull's Tornadoes?**

➡ **What is the North Stand at Easter Road better known as?**

➡ **Apart from a football, what are the other three elements that make up the Club badge?**

➡ **From which Irish club did manager Pat Fenlon join Hibernian?**

➡ **Which junior club did Pat Stanton play for prior to making his Hibernian debut?**

Answers on page 58-59

Hibernian in the Community

It is not only on match days that Easter Road Stadium is a hub of community activity! Monday through to Friday, the South Stand is filled with people taking part in a wide range of activities offered by Hibernian Community Foundation. On a daily basis, the Foundation and Hibernian FC work together to provide even more ways for fans and supporters to be part of the sport and the Club they love.

The Hibernian Learning Centre is a state of the art computer suite where people of all ages can come to learn and gain valuable qualifications in IT. We work with Edinburgh College (formerly Jewel & Esk) to offer computer courses, where people can learn at their own pace in a welcoming and comfortable space. With options that include social media, digitisation, core computing, European Computer Driving Licence (ECDL), music composition and performance, digital photo albums, storyboarding and broadcast journalism, we offer courses that appeal to many different interests.

We also run programmes that focus on health and fitness for men, women and families. Organised around the principles of peak performance and healthy lifestyles, our courses help people understand what it takes to make a real and positive difference in their own lives and how to achieve personal goals while having fun along the way.

Hibernian grassroots football is growing and we are committed to increasing access and opportunity for children, young people and adults to receive quality coaching across Edinburgh and East Lothian. We have redeveloped our training and coaching to include progression and assessment along with playing opportunities for all abilities. We also work with local schools and clubs to make sure all young people have a chance to play and enjoy football.

HIBERNIAN COMMUNITY FOUNDATION

www.hibernianinthecom

Our approach is to work in partnerships with others and to add value to activities and initiatives through the power and passion of football.

Along with our partnerships with Edinburgh College and the Scottish FA, we have partnerships with:

TCMO/Xpress Recruiting to support people into employment;

Lothian Special Olympics to support the Lothian Hibernian disability football team by providing regular coaching with assistance from the Hibernian Football Club's Under 19 squad;

East Lothian and City of Edinburgh Councils helping primary school pupils connect with the history, science, culture and management of sport through Hibernian Learning Initiatives.

We continue to work with volunteers and partners to develop new activities and programmes that meet different needs. Hibernian fans and supporters are the keys to our success and individual and corporate donations provide vital support in the form of time, energy, ideas and money. We are grateful for your generosity and commitment to efforts to improve health, promote learning and enhance opportunity in our community.

unity.org.uk

A is for Atherton – Bobby Atherton played for Hibernian in the late 19th century after joining from rivals Hearts. He was the Club's only player to be capped by Wales, and in 1902 captained the Club in the Scottish Cup win.

B is for the Baker Boy – the great striker Joe Baker, capped by England, and the holder of all kinds of Hibernian scoring records including nine in one game against Peebles Rovers in a Scottish Cup tie. Two spells at Hibernian for a true legend.

C is for Combe – often described as the sixth member of the great Famous Five. Bobby Combe was a versatile and talented footballer and was also Club captain. He gave 16 years of fantastic service and was capped three times by Scotland.

D is for Duncan – Arthur Duncan and the flying wide man was a star of the Turnbull's Tornadoes. He scored 112 goals for the Club during his career, which also brought him six caps.

E is for Edwards – Alex Edwards was the midfield brains in the Tornadoes side, and played an integral part in the seven goal demolition of rivals Hearts at New Year's Day in 1973.

F is for Famous Five – the greatest forward line the Scottish Game has ever seen; Smith, Johnstone, Reilly, Turnbull and Ormond. League titles won in the most cavalier fashion, and fame throughout Europe and beyond. The greatest Hibernian side of all time.

G is for Gordon – Alan Gordon was an elegant and intelligent centre forward in the early 1970s. A qualified accountant once famously told by manager Eddie Turnbull "The problem with you, son, is all your brains are in your head."

H is for Hamilton – Willie Hamilton was a frustrating genius, prodigiously talented and often wayward but always a real entertainer at his peak in the 1960s.

I is for Internationalists – Lawrie Reilly remains player to have won most caps whilst a Hibernian player, with 38 caps for the great Famous Five centre forward.

J is for Jackson – Darren Jackson scored 50 goals in 173 appearances for Hibernian in the 1990s, and improved both his attitude and his physical strength and pace through hard work and dedication.

K is for Kinloch – Bobby Kinloch will be forever remembered as the man who scored the winning goal when Hibernian defeated mighty Barcelona in a nail biting and ill-tempered Fairs Cup tie at Easter Road in the 1960/61 season.

L is for Latapy – Russell Latapy, the little magician from Trinidad, was the entertainer in chief with Frank Sauzee as Alex McLeish's Hibernian lit up Scottish football. The little attacking midfielder terrified Hearts, and helped consign the Tynecastle side to several memorable defeats

M is for McCartney – the elegantly attired Hibernian manager Willie McCartney had the vision to create the Famous Five team in the 1940s and tragically died before seeing them land the league title.

N is for Ned – no man has provided greater service to the Club than Eddie "Ned" Turnbull. As a player, he was a key part of the Famous Five, the club's greatest ever team. As manager, he coached Turnbull's Tornadoes to more success as arguably the second best team in the Club's history.

O is for O'Rourke – Jimmy O'Rourke, Hibernian fan and player, his nose for a goal and his love for the club ensured he was always a favourite. In the talented Tornadoes side, he was a real spark.

P is for Preston North End – Hibernian defeated the English Club in a match billed as the Association Football Championship of the World decider in 1897. Hibernian won, the Scottish Cup holders defeating the side that would become known as The Invincibles.

Q is for Quinn – Pat Quinn joined Hibernian in 1963, the midfield schemer starring under managers Jock Stein and Bob Shankly.

R is for Roughie – Alan Rough, goalkeeper with more than 50 caps to his name, joined Hibernian from Partick Thistle and stayed for five seasons, his calmness and ability ensuring he ranks among the Club's goalkeeping heroes.

S is for Sauzee – Frank Sauzee, known to the Hibernian family simply as Le God. The Frenchman was a European Cup Winner when Alex McLeish brought him to the Club. It proved brilliant business. Even in the twilight of his career, an inspirational player and leader. Hibernian never lost to Hearts when Sauzee played.

T is for Templeton – Bobby Templeton played for Hibernian as a defender for sixteen years from 1911, and also managed the Club until 1935.

HIBERNIAN F.C.—1933-34.
Back Row (Left to right):—LANGTON, WILKINSON, BLYTH, URQUHART, WATSON, CRAWFORD.

U is for Urquhart – Duncan Urquhart played from 1928 till 1935, the full-back earning a Scotland cap for his tough tackling performances.

V is for Victory – the thrashing of Hearts at Tynecastle on New Year's Day, 1973, remains the biggest margin of victory in an Edinburgh derby.

W is for Whelahan – Michael Whelahan was the first ever man to Captain Hibernian FC when he helped found the Club in 1875. The Hibernian legend that is Pat Stanton is a descendant of the Club's first captain.

X marks the spot – Hibernian remain the penalty shoot-out kings of Scottish football, having never lost to another Scottish side in this way.

Y is for Younger – Tommy Younger was a gentle giant, but he was also a goalkeeper of great ability as demonstrated by the 24 caps he earned. He kept goal for the trip championship winning Famous Five team.

Z is for Zitelli – the stylish Frenchman was a friend and team-mate of Frank Sauzee, his gift for spectacular goals including a stunning overhead strike and a thunderous goal in a Uefa Cup tie at Easter Road.

FOOTBALL PLAYED HERE
ST. MIRREN FOOTBALL CLUB
John
M5
CRABBIE'S
CRABBIE'S
10

ton
Gra
Wardrop
INDEPENDENT
FINANCIAL ADVISE
0141 226 3184
M6

PLAYERS QUIZ

➦ **Which long-serving player had a testimonial last season?**

➦ **Which current Hibernian player has skippered Scotland's U-21 side?**

➦ **Which young Hibernian striker scored two goals to knock Hearts out of the Youth Cup?**

➦ **Where did Eoin Doyle score his first goal for Hibs?**

➦ **Which current Hibernian player was man of the match in the 2007 League Cup final win over Kilmarnock?**

➦ **Which country does Jorge Claros represent?**

Answers on page 58-59

HIBS KIDS

All HIBS KIDS memberships include all the usual benefits:

➡ Unique Hibs Kids Membership Card

➡ 4 free SPL games for non-ticket members

➡ Discounts for Green Shoots football training courses - staged at Hibernian Training Centre beside the first team squad!

➡ 15% discount at the Hibernian on Hibs Kids Days

➡ Season Ticket Members 'Bring a Friend' concessions on 2012/13 Hibs Kids Days!

➡ Hibs Kids Christmas Panto (0-8 years)

➡ Hibs Kids Football Tournament (9-11 years)

➡ Birthday Card

MATCHDAY FUN!

Hibs Kids also provides the chance for members to get closer to their Club with regular FREE draws to take part in Mascot, Ball Person and '10 Second Challenge' selection.

For more information, visit the club website at
www.hibernianfc.co.uk

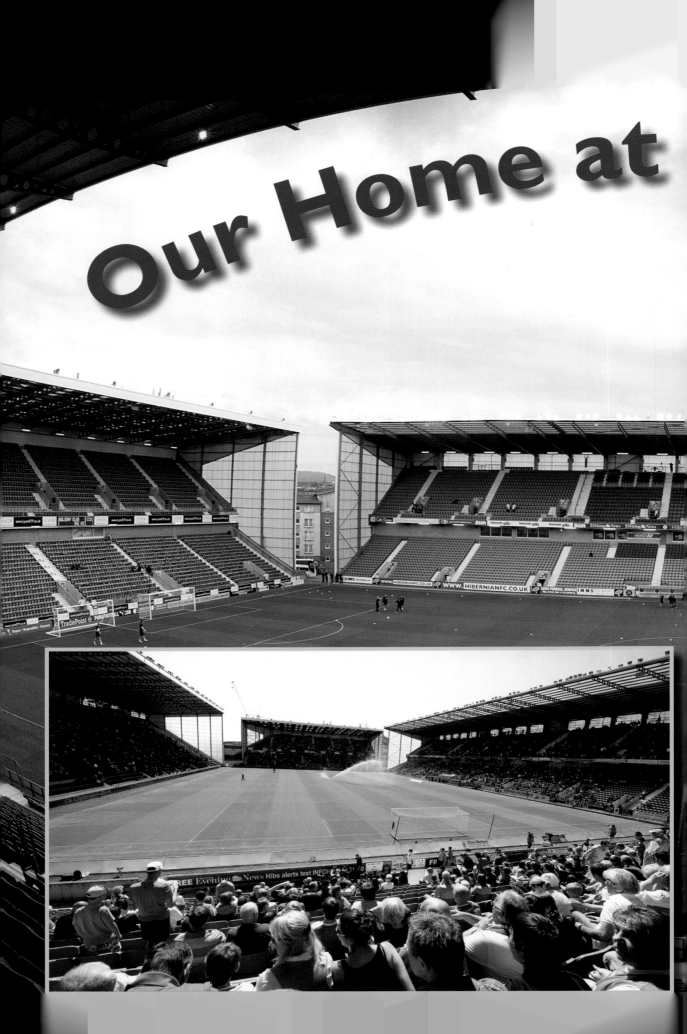

Our Home at

EASTER ROAD

Preserving
a Glorious History

Since its earliest days Hibernian FC has been a trailblazer for Scottish football, and has a rich and varied history, be it the first British team to compete in European competition or the Scottish side to play under floodlights or utilise undersoil heating. The task of preserving and presenting that wonderful history is carried out superbly well by the Hibernian Historical Trust, a proactive initiative by both supporters and the Club. Formed by a group of supporters including club historian Tom Wright, the legally recognised Trust has been created totally independently from the Football Club but with the full backing of the Board. Hibernian Football Club has donated its entire and considerable collection of artefacts and memorabilia to the Trust. The Trust is always keen to obtain Hibernian-related items, either on a permanent basis or on loan, and anyone in possession of items of interest is encouraged to contact the Trust.

The Trust's achievements include: -

- Restoring and rededicating club founder Canon Hannan's Memorial;

- Remounting and rededicating the commemorative plaque to former chairman Harry Swan;

- Installing plaques and display boards to the Famous Five outside the Famous Five Stand;

- Decorating 'Behind the Goals' in the Famous Five Stand;

- The purchase of the 1887 Scottish Cup Winners Medal presented to Jerry Reynolds;

- The purchase of the 1906 Scottish International Cap won by George Stewart;

- The purchase of the 1947 Scottish League jersey belonging to Davy Shaw; and

- The commissioning of the James Main Plaque, located in the lower concourse of the Famous Five Stand.

If you can assist the Trust in obtaining items which would help us in this quest, or you would like to contribute an item, either permanently or on loan, the Trust would be delighted to hear from you.

In addition, you can also help financially. The Trust is always grateful to receive financial assistance from individuals, supporters' clubs and businesses. As a registered charity (No. SC035683) the Gift Aid scheme run by the government allows the Trust to reclaim 25% tax on every eligible donation from a UK taxpayer, making each donation go further. Further information online at www.hibshistoricaltrust.org.uk

TOP MEN
Between The Posts

Hibernian has enjoyed the services of some superb goalkeepers over the years, and this year we take the opportunity to look at some of fine shot-stoppers who made up a golden period for Hibernian in the modern era.

Alan Rough played 175 times for Hibernian after signing from Partick Thistle in 1982, and earned 53 caps during his long career. He played in two World Cups, and has the honour of being named in Pat Stanton's Dream Team. The perm-haired keeper's amiable sense of humour often distracted from his quality as a goalkeeper, but a place in the Scotland Hall of Fame with more than 50 caps is no mean achievement.

Andy Goram was to take Roughie's place between the sticks at Easter Road when he signed from Oldham in 1987. He went on to play 138 times for the Hibees – his father had kept goal for Hibs in the past - before earning a £1 million move to Ibrox and Rangers. Goram was a huge success at Hibs, and has the distinction of scoring in a league match at Morton. He played 43 times for Scotland, and also represented his country at cricket!

Goram's move west saw an even bigger character take over the gloves at Easter Road with the arrival of **John "Budgie" Burridge** in 1991. The man from the north of England became an instant cult hero for his eccentricities, but he was also a very considerable goalie and was part of a Hibs team that landed the Skol League Cup in 1991. Much travelled, Budgie was much admired and much liked at Easter Road.

Jim Leighton arrived in 1993 at Hibernian. Jim, who made his stellar reputation with Alex Ferguson's Aberdeen side, had endured an unhappy few years down south following an ill-starred move following his old gaffer to Manchester. His star renewed at Hibernian, where his fantastic performances in his 151 appearances for the Club saw him recalled to the Scotland team. Jim remains Scotland's most-capped keeper, with 91 international appearances. He left the club in 1997 to return to Aberdeen.

SPOT THE BALL

Can you guess which ball is in the correct spot?
Answers on page 58-59

Spotlight
on Paul Hanlon

He's represented his country at under 19 and under 21 level – as skipper – and has captained his Club at the tender age of 20. Paul Hanlon has shown that he is not only a player with a big future in the game – he's a leader to boot.

Paul, now aged 22, is a product of the vaunted Hibernian Academy, and made an early breakthrough into the Hibernian first team squad from a youth team which won a League and Cup double. A talented and composed defender, he plays at centre back or left back.

A quiet, modest young man, Paul is nonetheless passionate about the Club, he not only plays for, but supports. He said: "If I wasn't playing I'd be in the stand watching – I was brought up a Hibs supporter and I know what the fans go through and what they feel."

He played his first senior game way back in January 2008, against Inverness Caledonian Thistle, standing in for the injured David Murphy at left back. The following season saw him make a few starts, but since then, he has been in regular top team action.

Paul has also played regularly for his country, and skippered the national side at under 21 level where he has gained more than 20 caps and scored two goals.

" If I wasn't playing I'd be in the stand watching – I was brought up a Hibs supporter and I know what the fans go through and what they feel. "

He began his career, as many players have, at the successful Edinburgh youth football club Hutchison Vale. In those early days, Paul was an attacking midfielder who scored goals, but he was converted to a defensive position after he signed for Hibernian.

Paul's abilities have been talked up by several coaches and managers – even when things have not been going smoothly for Hibernian. Billy Stark, his boss at under

21 level, said of his captain: "Sir Alex Ferguson often used adversity to find out about a young player, his character and so on. It can often make or break a young player.

"He would see if you could handle it and if you couldn't you were no use to him. If you could you had his total trust. Paul has had some tough times at Easter Road but it has been character forming for him and he has been outstanding for Hibs.

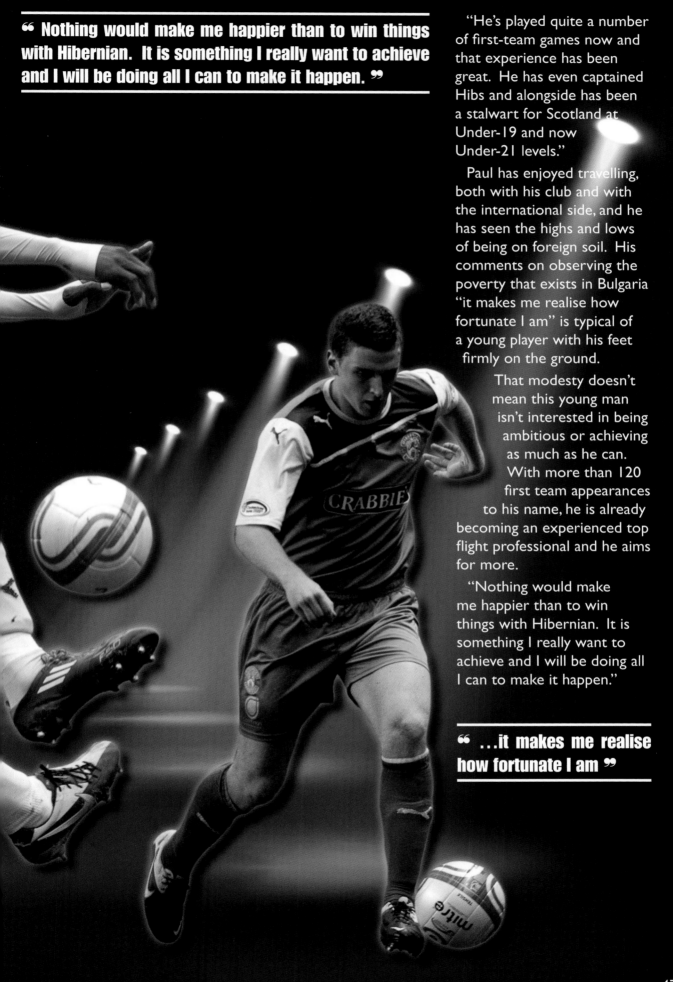

❝ Nothing would make me happier than to win things with Hibernian. It is something I really want to achieve and I will be doing all I can to make it happen. ❞

"He's played quite a number of first-team games now and that experience has been great. He has even captained Hibs and alongside has been a stalwart for Scotland at Under-19 and now Under-21 levels."

Paul has enjoyed travelling, both with his club and with the international side, and he has seen the highs and lows of being on foreign soil. His comments on observing the poverty that exists in Bulgaria "it makes me realise how fortunate I am" is typical of a young player with his feet firmly on the ground.

That modesty doesn't mean this young man isn't interested in being ambitious or achieving as much as he can. With more than 120 first team appearances to his name, he is already becoming an experienced top flight professional and he aims for more.

"Nothing would make me happier than to win things with Hibernian. It is something I really want to achieve and I will be doing all I can to make it happen."

❝ ...it makes me realise how fortunate I am ❞

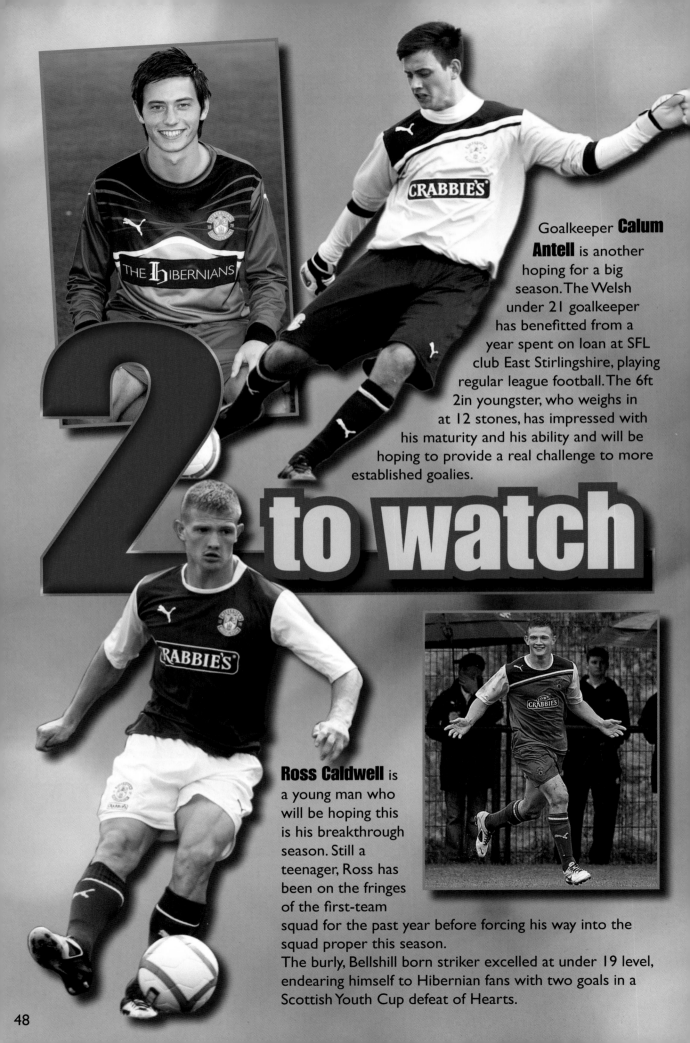

2 to watch

Goalkeeper **Calum Antell** is another hoping for a big season. The Welsh under 21 goalkeeper has benefitted from a year spent on loan at SFL club East Stirlingshire, playing regular league football. The 6ft 2in youngster, who weighs in at 12 stones, has impressed with his maturity and his ability and will be hoping to provide a real challenge to more established goalies.

Ross Caldwell is a young man who will be hoping this is his breakthrough season. Still a teenager, Ross has been on the fringes of the first-team squad for the past year before forcing his way into the squad proper this season.

The burly, Bellshill born striker excelled at under 19 level, endearing himself to Hibernian fans with two goals in a Scottish Youth Cup defeat of Hearts.

10 FACTS
ABOUT LEWIS STEVENSON

- Lewis will be 25 in January 2012.
- He was born and educated in Kirkcaldy, Fife.
- He joined the Hibernian Academy aged 14.
- Lewis is 5ft 7ins tall.
- His competitive debut came in a League Cup win in September 2005.
- He was Man of the Match in the 5-1 League Cup Final victory over Kilmarnock in 2007.
- He has 8 caps for Scotland at under 21 level.
- He scored his only goal for Hibernian to date in 2011 against Inverness.
- He has made more than 120 appearances for the first team.
- Lewis is currently the club's longest serving player.

COLOURING IN PAGE

Show your support for Hibernian's green and white traditions by colouring in this image of striker Danny Handling, one of the team's youngest ever players.

NEW HIBEES

Irishman **Tim Clancy** was the **Manager's** first signing of the summer transfer window, when he joined from fellow **SPL** side Motherwell on a two-year deal.

The 28-year-old versatile defender can play across the back four, and was an integral part of Motherwell's successful season last year. He gave up the chance of European football to sign on at Easter Road, saying he jumped at the opportunity to join "a big Club in Scotland."

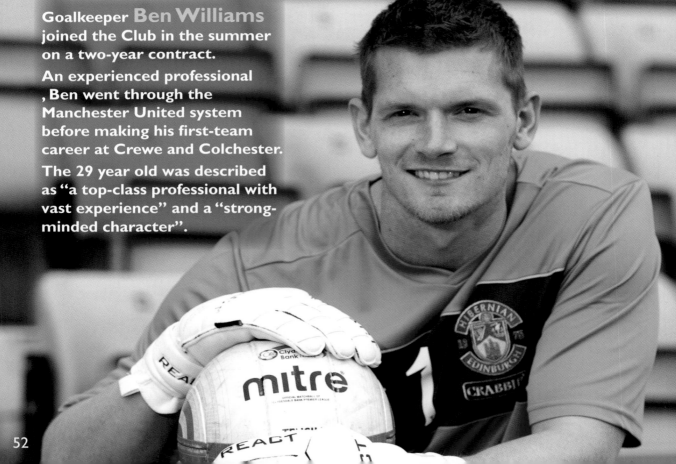

Goalkeeper **Ben Williams** joined the **Club** in the summer on a two-year contract.

An experienced professional, Ben went through the **Manchester United** system before making his first-team career at Crewe and Colchester.

The 29 year old was described as "a top-class professional with vast experience" and a "strong-minded character".

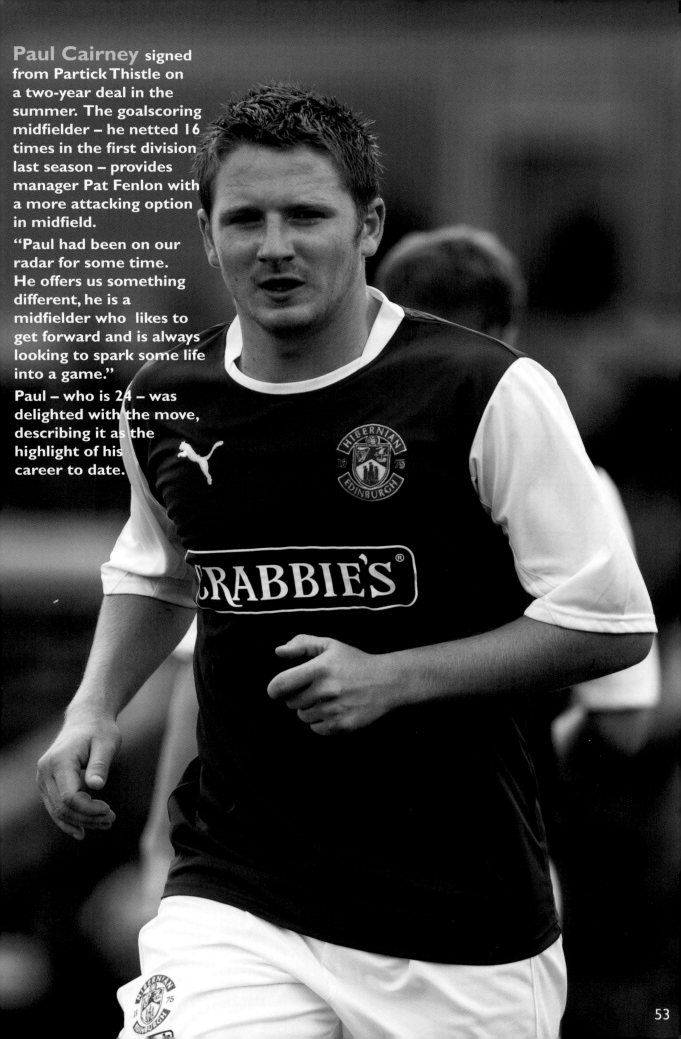

Paul Cairney signed from Partick Thistle on a two-year deal in the summer. The goalscoring midfielder – he netted 16 times in the first division last season – provides manager Pat Fenlon with a more attacking option in midfield.

"Paul had been on our radar for some time. He offers us something different, he is a midfielder who likes to get forward and is always looking to spark some life into a game."

Paul – who is 24 – was delighted with the move, describing it as the highlight of his career to date.

Wordsearch

Can you find the names of these
Hibs goalscorers in the grid below?

Find the words in the grid.

Words can go horizontally, vertically and
diagonally in all eight directions.

Q	X	N	L	N	O	D	R	O	G	Z
N	H	A	M	H	L	S	M	J	N	Q
N	K	D	A	Q	T	T	T	C	N	Q
O	C	R	R	N	H	I	O	E	R	Q
S	T	O	T	G	F	R	M	E	I	L
K	K	I	I	L	M	W	I	S	G	N
C	N	R	N	A	K	L	R	H	R	K
A	W	R	C	H	L	K	N	E	H	D
J	M	K	L	Y	C	L	K	C	J	L
R	Q	D	U	N	C	A	N	R	R	W
B	B	D	L	A	B	I	H	C	R	A

Archibald	Gordon	Riordan
Baker	Jackson	Smith
Cormack	Martin	Stein
Duncan	Reilly	Wright

Answers on page 58-59

Hibernian Ladies

Hibernian Girls and Ladies scored a major coup when they announced that TV star, Kirsty Gallacher, was to become their patron.

The popular sports presenter is the daughter of lifelong Hibernian fan Bernard Gallacher – better known as a top professional golfer and victorious Ryder Cup skipper.

Hibernian Ladies has been one of the strongest team's in Scottish Women's Football since their founding in 1999 – having won all the domestic honours.

In season 2006/7, the Ladies broke new records, going an entire league season without dropping a single point and winning the Scottish Cup in emphatic style with a 5-1 victory over Glasgow City.

This season saw the Ladies get off to a promising start, at the time of writing with many big wins recorded and only three defeats.

Hibernian Ladies runs three teams, the A squad, Hibernian Ladies 2000 and Hibernian Ladies 1875, as well as girls squads at under 17, under 15 and under 13 level.

Hibernian Histo

Sir Tom Farmer

History at a glance

- Founded in 1875 by members of the Catholic Young Men's Society attached to St Patrick's Church in Edinburgh's "Little Ireland" – the Cowgate.

- The name derives from Latin and means Irishmen.

- Scottish Cup winners in 1887, and a defeat of Preston North End the same year saw Hibernian crowned "World Club Champions".

- Greatest era – The Famous Five years in the 1950s which secured league championships and saw Hibernian as the first British Club to compete in the European Cup, losing at the semi-final stage.

- A second golden era during the 1970s when "Turnbull's Tornadoes" won silverware and played thrilling football.

- Attempted takeover by Hearts owner Wallace Mercer in 1990 as Hibernian faces financial melt-down.

- Present owner Sir Tom Farmer CBE saves the Club from extinction, and a League Cup win follows shortly after in 1991.

- Stadium redeveloped in 1990s and at the turn of the decade.

- Hibernian wins League Cup in 5-1 win over Kilmarnock in March 2007.

- Club opens Hibernian Training Centre in December 2007.

- Stadium redevelopment completed with opening of new East Stand, summer 2010.

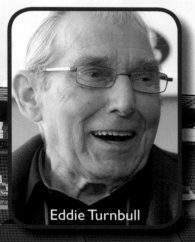
Eddie Turnbull

Honours

Scottish League Winners (4)	1902/03, 1947/48, 1950/51, 1951/52
First Division winners (2)	1980/81, 1998/99
Division Two winners (3)	1893/94, 1894/95, 1932/33
Division One runners-up (6)	1896/97, 1946/47, 1949/50, 1952/53, 1973/74, 1974/75
Scottish Cup winners (2)	1887, 1902
Scottish Cup runners-up (10)	1896, 1914, 1923, 1924, 1947, 1958, 1972, 1979, 2001, 2012
Scottish League Cup winners (3)	1972/73, 1991/92, 2006/07
Scottish League Cup runners-up (6)	1950/51, 1968/69, 1974/75, 1985/86, 1993/94, 2003/04
Drybrough Cup winners (2)	1972/73, 1973/74
Summer Cup winners (2)	1941, 1964

QUIZ ANSWERS

Season Quiz p12

Pat Fenlon
Leigh Griffiths
O'Connor and Griffiths
McPake
Mark Brown
Gambia
Northern Ireland

Quiz p20

Michael Whelahan
Eddie Turnbull and Pat Stanton
Famous Five Stand
The Harp, the Castle and the Ship
Bohemians
Bonnyrigg Rose

Players Quiz p34

Ian Murray
Paul Hanlon
Ross Caldwell
Cowdenbeath
Lewis Stevenson
Hondur

QUIZ ANSWERS

Spot the Ball p42

Wordsearch p54

Club Contacts

General Enquiries
club@hibernianfc.co.uk
Tel: 0131 661 2159

Corporate & Commercial Manager
Russell Smith
rsmith@hibernianfc.co.uk
0131 656 7072

Match-day Sales Manager
Amanda Vettese
avettese@hibernianfc.co.uk
Tel: 0131 656 7073

Media Manager
Andrew Sleight
asleight@hibernianfc.co.uk
0131 656 7079

Ticket Operations
Judith Ireland
Ticket Office Manager
jireland@hibernianfc.co.uk
Tel: 0844 844 1875 (Option 2)

Conference & Banqueting
All Enquiries to:
Tel: 0131 656 7075

Where's Sunshine the Leith Lynx?